# MOURNING DOVE

## Dream Poems

# MOURNING DOVE

## Dream Poems

Patricia Garfield, Ph.D.

Author of *Creative Dreaming*

2013 Reprint Edition published by

Dr. Patricia Garfield's Center for Creative Dreaming
www.CreativeDreaming.org

ISBN of 2013 Reprint Edition: 978-0615853055

First published by Numina Books, Pt. Reyes, CA.

*MOURNING DOVE: Dream Poems*
©2007, Patricia Garfield, Ph.D.

Book Design and Production: Linda Corwin/Avantgraphics

All paintings are by the author from her book
*Pathway to Ecstasy: The Way of the Dream Mandala*
(Holt, Rinehart & Winston, 1979; Prentice Hall, 1989).

*Credits for photographs:*
Photo of author and husband (page 13) by Don Crowe, 2002;
photos of author as child (pages 36 and 42) by author's father, F. C. Goff;
photo of author behind web (page 44) by her brother, F. M. Goff, 2005;
photo of author (page 52) by her husband, Zal Garfield, 1972;
photo of author (back cover) by Fariba Bogzaran, 2006.

Library of Congress Catalog data available on request.

Printed in the U.S.A.

*In memory of Zal,*
*    who opened*
*        his loving heart . . .*

# OTHER BOOKS
## BY
## PATRICIA GARFIELD

Creative Dreaming

Pathway to Ecstasy:
The Way of the Dream Mandala

Your Child's Dreams

Women's Bodies, Women's Dreams

The Healing Power of Dreams

The Dream Messenger:
How Dreams of the Departed Bring Healing Gifts

The Universal Dream Key:
The Twelve Most Common Dream Themes Around the World

The Dream Book:
A Young Person's Guide to Understanding Dreams

Dream Catcher:
A Young Person's Journal for Exploring Dreams

# CONTENTS

# ILLUSTRATIONS

*10 paintings*
*7 photographs*

# SPECIAL THANKS

Learning a new skill requires the input of various mentors. My special thanks go to poets Margaret Kaufman, John Savant, and Thomas Centolella, who guided my faltering early steps. I'm grateful to artist Fariba Bogzaran and Ted Cousens who encouraged making this book.

Other friends and family, even those who "don't get" poetry were loving and supportive as I struggled with finding the way to express and cope with loss. Heartfelt appreciation to these dear people, who know who they are.

# FOREWORD

Since the death of my beloved husband, Zal, on August 3, 2002, I have explored many avenues to assuage my grief. Having been happily married for more than thirty-three years, I felt that losing Zal was like being ripped in half.

He was born on a Valentine's Day, destined to be a loving person. We had been colleagues in a clinical psychology doctoral program, became best friends, lovers, and eventually soulmates. We wrote professional papers together, traveled the world, read aloud to one another, and shared an intimacy that is rare.

In my state of devastation following Zal's death, I underwent individual grief counseling, attended grief groups, and art therapy groups. I participated in a health immersion program. These therapeutic activities helped, as did the support of friends and family. Yet, I still felt stricken.

After the first anniversary of Zal's death I wept for two weeks solid. My eyelids became so swollen that when they finally receded, the top layer of skin peeled off. Deciding that this state of mind had to stop, I started responding to requests for dates. The subsequent dating experiences were decidedly mixed, but they provided a distraction, as did throwing myself into work projects that resulted in the publication of two books for teens on the subject of dreams.

Beyond all the efforts I made to re-center myself, I found the greatest relief in studying poetry. Within its structured language, I discovered a container for my sorrow. When I tried to write about my grief in a free form, I was overwhelmed by it; I found it difficult to turn off or even slow its flow. However, when I cast my distress into the pre-determined shape of a poetic form, weeping as I wrote, splashing tears all over the keyboard, the sadness came to an end with the final line. When I reread the finished piece, I'd cry again, yet I could let the tears conclude. Poetry gave me a vessel capable of holding grief.

Poetry has been described as "the highest and most complex form of human speech" (by poet and teacher Michael J. Bugeja in *The Art and Craft of Poetry*). As I explored this craft, in workshops and in literature, I learned how many creative people of past times have struck upon the same therapeutic effect of poetry. I followed the trail of those who had suffered centuries ago, as well as today, and felt a kinship with the wounded, some of whom had lost far more than a cherished mate.

Gradually I began to notice the similarity between dreams (my area of expertise) and the content of poems. They both cast emotion into the shape of images; they both deal in metaphor; they both provide clues as to how to live well despite loss.

In *Mourning Dove*, I try to share this knowledge with readers, with the hope that you, too, may find solace and inspiration. Love, like physical energy, may shift shape but lives on, eternally . . .

Patricia Garfield
*Tiburon, California, February 14, 2007*

*Patricia and Zal a few short months prior to Zal's death.*

night of Friday
3/9/73

San Francisco

*[margin: sleep about 12:00]*

I am with a group of professionals at a conference. We are discussing various aspects of dreaming. Several people have spoken earlier of the symbolism involved in "leaving," referring to leaves dropping from a tree. Zal + I are seated on chairs at the front. All of us are eating. I stand up and say, "We've talked about 'leaving,' I'd like to discuss the concept 'branching.' I've had several dreams in which there was a growth. There was a woman's head and from it grew branches, almost like antlers, but many, more and more, each subdividing until it grew very thick, dense." I describe more + more, feeling invested + excited. I finish + there is a slight pause as the head person, to whom I've mainly addressed the remarks, gets up, and ducks under a kind of table top in front of her to get more food. Meantime, Zal says to me, "You did that really well," and kisses me on the cheek. People get distracted with the arrival of more food + begin to eat. I don't get any response other than Zal's. This is frustrating but I still feel good from expressing myself. They are now distributing various kinds of cake. By the time they get to the table where I am now, there are only a few wedges left. I express a preference for one type but don't think I get it. There are several pieces on one plate, some to be shared with a blonde girl next to me. I just begin to eat without waiting further. One piece of cake is rather like crushed pineapple. I eat what I want.

*[margin right: Zal is "leaving" again on Sunday on business trip — like trees in fall]*
*[margin right: Did I dream this before?]*
*[margin right: Cher + I had baked cake for party]*
*[margin right: Seno say you should share food]*
*[margin right: I like crushed pineapple]*

*[margin: wake 7:00]*

(vague recall) Before — I'm with the same group. Zal + I are seated closely on a bench or the floor, touching. Zal is talking to someone about a baby brother. I look into a mirror and hold my hair up. I look well that way I'll have to try it after I shower. Then I let some fall down in a piece near each cheek. It looks even prettier. I wear a long skirt. I am surprised how I'd thought there was nothing from the freedom movement I wanted for myself. There actually were some things like this I'd enjoy changing and experimenting with. My hair was long + wavy. I'd have to let it grow longer.

*[margin right: I want to buy a long skirt]*
*[margin right: theme of growing things branches. hair]*

Facts — A very full day. Straightened house, worked at desk *[working on book]* in morning. Ran several errands downtown in afternoon. Dinner with Mama + Cher. Drove out to airport to meet Zal. Zal tired from hectic trip, but both feeling very loving. Had welcome home party with cake. Made love.

# Dream
# Notes

The poems in this section are drawn from specific dream imagery. In the case of "Branching Woman," I have included a reproduction of the original dream journal entry (shown opposite) as well as my Chinese brush painting of the same name. Both served as inspiration for the poem. While painting a central dream image, the dreamer engages in a unique form of meditation on its meaning. Writing a poem about this same image extends the dreamer's undestanding.

"Spirit Bird" and "She" are also accompanied by paintings I made of their subjects. "A Poem for Strength" and "At Night," likewise, are founded on my actual dream experiences.

[Note: All the Chinese brush paintings included in these pages first appeared in my book *Pathway to Ecstasy: The Way of the Dream Mandala*.]

## Invocation to
## Branching Woman

Great Matriarch! Mother of dreamy
life paths that diverge and reach
like trees into the future, please hear me.

Come, as when I first saw you shake
your shimmering limbs to reveal
the finest course for me to take.

Full-crowned, your grand branches traced,
like antler-thoughts, the parting routes
feeling out the choices faced.

For decades I have followed where you led
while your gifts petal-showered down on me.
Now the light fades; the track grows shaded.

Hornèd Goddess, you nodded your royal head
to indicate the trail for ancient feet to tread;
don't leave me in confusion. Visit my dream-bed.

Blaze again, Mighty Mother! Stir your boughs.
Shake your horns. Point out the branch
to advance to fullest life that time allows.

Show me, I implore, the right way forward.

*January, 2007*

## SPIRIT BIRD

Last night I groomed my spirit bird
to make his plumage shine;
deftly I spread the oil from head
to tip of spine.

He sat content to let me preen
a glossy sheen on every feather,
protective shield to guard him
in every weather,

unlike those birds in dreams past
with ruffled barbs, unfed, or ill,
or on the bottom of the cage
ominously still.

Other dream birds, tame,
will perch upon my finger,
fly giddily around the room,
or play the singer,

but *this* bird bends to my touch,
ready to carry my reply
to a message I can't quite grasp,
some half-heard cry . . .

*February, 2005*

*Soaring to the Moon*

## SHE

I am She who skims the stormy waves
saving shipwrecked souls
from salty graves.

I am She who hovers over burial earth
pulsing fire-force from fingertips,
awaking women's birth.

I am She who dwells in dripping caves
weaving spells into my hair
with white flowers.

I am She who soars to the lustrous moon
and splashes in its sheen to renew
all spirit powers.

On sea, under ground, in fire or air,
you'll find me—guardian—always there.

*December, 2006*

## A Poem For Strength

"Give me a poem for strength,"
a small girl in my dream pleads.

I open the little box I hold
but see only tiny dolls.
I yearn to give her one,
yet it will make us sad.

I shake my head, no.
"You must!" she insists.

Sighing, I reply,
"My child, all you need
to dispel your fear is here:
Take this special doll,
clasp it close with care,
rock it tenderly,
comb its tangled hair."

I wonder if her soul remembers
how loving makes us whole?

*2006*

# At Night When I Put Out the Light

At night when I put out the light
a flame inside me blazes bright,
and as I slip into a pillowed sleep,
shapes arise to inner eyes
from some deep cavern that lies
far below, and steep.

A black horse gallops by,
his mane whipping high;
a wild bird lands upon my hand;
the flower-haired goddess, friend
in watery cave, bids me descend;
I step into a dripping land.

Two ravens on my shoulders perch
as guards who guide my search
for the rainbow snake
with jeweled crown
slithering down
the twisting path I take.

Creatures, thieves and lovers creep
along my corridors of sleep
toward me, their goal,
as I dream throughout the night—
'til daybreak splits their seeming might
and I awaken, shaken, but whole.

*2004*

*An anonymous ship photographer took this photograph of Zal and me walking on the Greek island of Hydra in 1972. It captures some of the joy we shared in each other's company.*

# Grief

The poems in this section on grief were composed at different stages of mourning during the nearly five years since Zal's death.

"Two Weeks After" is based on dream images shortly after my husbasnd died. "Open Secret," "Mourning Dove," (the title poem) and "The Teller and the Told" date from a later time frame; they do not involve dream imagery.

The poem "The Horses" draws upon dream images that occurred during the approximate first year after Zal's death. The horse painting that accompanies this poem comes from an earlier dream. "Shoulder Guide," with its painting of the Egyptian "soul bird," as well as the horse first appeared in *Pathway*.

## Two Weeks After Your Death

Two weeks after your death,
I dreamed I lay in a wooden box,
wailing.

Then, I kept sweeping shattered glass,
weeping.

Where are you?

*August, 2002*

## OPEN SECRET

You sat at your desk, working cheerfully.
I drove to market and back in an hour flat;
You said, "I thought you abandoned me."
I bit my lip, "I'd *never* do that!"

Your aging face, I saw, was pale with dread—
after that, I took you with me everywhere.
At Book Passage, you drank tea and read;
at Whole Foods, you chewed a juicy pear.

In Open Secret, you slumped in an armchair
with *Sexual Ecstasy* to explore,
"How is it?" I asked, surprised; "Good," you declared;
soon, you nodded over it, asleep, a-snore.

One week more: you died clutching me, your touchstone;
but O, my love, you did not die alone.

*August, 2006*

## The Teller and the Told

Remember how, as your hearing faded,
our theater nights differed, for mine
was the only voice you still understood?
In the lobby before the show you'd get
a listening device that never did much good.

We'd watch Act One from the 8th row aisle
and, back to the lobby on intermission,
you'd ask, "What the *hell* was that all about?"
I, who love to tell tales, would explain how
the girl in the red party dress, the knockout,

was the secret lover of the man in the gray suit
who was married to the frizzy-haired blonde—
but they hadn't had sex in a long time
and she took up with the skinny guy who'd
given her a napkin note when she served wine,

and now the mess would spill as husband (he
of the gray suit) noticed the napkin swap;
and the newcomer (young woman in blue)
was the long-lost daughter of the lover's
(red dress) earlier marriage to a duke.

We'd return to our seats for Act Two,
satisfied or stunned, and repeat the process,
adjusting for costume changes because she,
lover, was now in a green suit (red dress
in Act One), recapping all before Act Three.

The whole drive home I wrapped up loose ends,
with tasty tidbits of the frizzy blonde's deceit;
the teller and the told, fulfilling each other's needs.
We put out the lights and slid under the sheet
with sighs, having seen/heard a good play.

Now that *your* curtain's fallen, my love,
stories pile high; expect, on the day
we meet again, to hear epic tales.
Costume alert: I'll wear an older body suit.
You'll know me by my stories, if all else fails.

*November, 2006*

## THE HORSES

Ten days
after you died,
I dreamed of horses strung
from nets in trees, suspended
alive,
I woke
teary-eyed.

Nine months later,
I saw mist
clearing
and above
on a mountainside
a black horse
running.

At a year,
I order
a horse
hitched to a carriage
for a journey
and fetch
the gear.

Soon, I
stride
into a stable,
see a horse being saddled
for a race, but not yet
ready
to ride.

Over a year
since you died,
I dream-spied a girl
in a white dress
on a white horse;
I catch
her eye.

*November, 2006*

## MOURNING DOVE

Standing by the kitchen window,
waiting for the water to boil,
I watch two doves mate
on the wooden railing.

He, taller, bluer, stretches high,
she, smaller, browner, bows low;
both weave their necks to and fro.

She coos feather-soft and he feeds her;
she waggles her silky tail and he
climbs above, crouches and thrusts.

The kettle whistles, the birds fly off;
I pour tea, cradle the steaming cup
in chilly fingers, carry it to the table.

Sitting in my bathrobe I stare
across the space at your empty chair.

*March, 2006*

## SHOULDER GUIDE

Do you remember the parakeet I had—
the blue one, sweet and tame?
He'd fly to me when I called his name,
alight and

ride on my left shoulder, nibbling
at my earlobe, or chewing on
a strand of hair and singing softly
in my ear.

In time, he grew sick and died, a short
yet pleasant life. I missed his silky
presence there, murmuring
in my ear.

Your life was long and happy, love, yet
you've flown, too. I sometimes wish
your spirit sat in his place, whispering
in my ear.

I'd listen to your words of comfort
and pretend I could ask your advice
on anything; you'd murmur wisely
and I would hear . . .

*January, 2007*

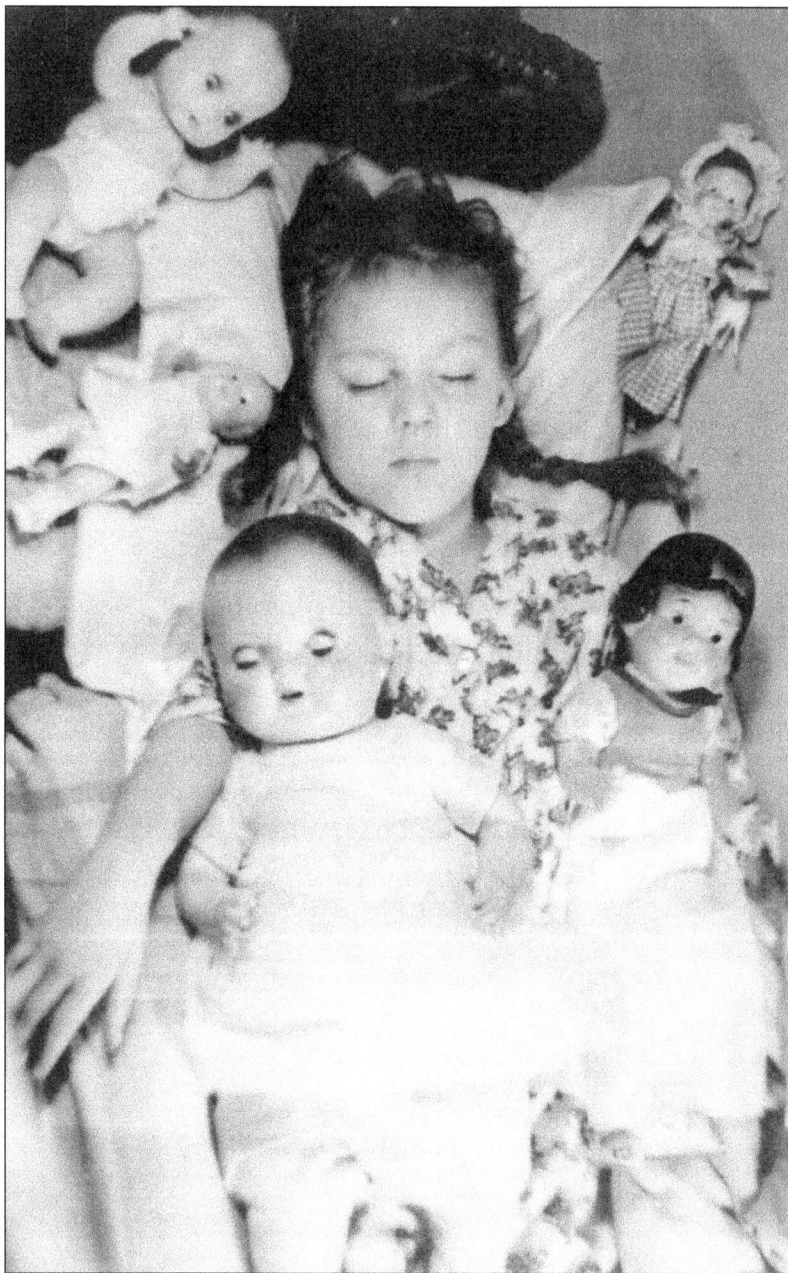

*My father took this photograph when I was about five or six years old. I was genuinely asleep, but he probably arranged my dolls. On the ceiling above my head, he had glued luminous stars and a moon that I fondly gazed at as I drifted to sleep.*

# Childhood

Although I didn't start a dream journal until I was fourteen, I do recall a few dreams from early childhood. In one, I was in a small plane; when it fell from the sky, I fell out of bed. I remember other dreams of flying, from the same time period, sailing through the air like Superman.

In my memory, the years through most of grade school were golden. "Marshmallow," "After School," and "Come Back, Maria Montez" reflect those near-magical times. The photograph of my brother and me that follows the Maria Montez poem gives a sense of the enchantment we were immersed in with Father's art and Mother's stories.

"The House on Willow Grove Avenue" depicts my emotional crisis when we moved into a different home. On the brink of puberty, I felt plunged into a murky and thorny environment. During this phase of life my parents' marriage grew troubled. They divorced after my brother and I left home, but remarried each other five years later. Talk about confusing!

## MARSHMALLOW

When I hold my stick just so
above the firelight's
wobbly glow
and turn it round and round
quite slow,
the white lump on the tip
will grow
all golden brown.

And when I bite into
its crispy crust
and taste the soft
center burst
into a warm, gushy mess,
it's the best
of all desserts!

*2004*

## AFTER SCHOOL
## After R. L. Stevenson

After school when homework's done
I dash outside to have some fun;
on the grass under the shady oak
I arrange my little folk.

Pipe-cleaner people with threads for hair
hop from the box I carry there—
a princess with golden locks, a dark queen,
Tarzan and heroes from films I've seen.

Across grass tundra-lawn they roam
to reach their jungle-flower home;
hands bent, they swing, stalk to stalk
to track the wild bug-beast's walk.

On leaf-beds beneath blossom-lights,
their coiled heads go to sleep at "nights."
Capture, rescue, hunt, and play
the hours simply melt away.

Lily-of-the-valley scents the air,
dappled sunlight dances everywhere.
Up root-mountains my people climb . . .
'til Mother calls "It's dinner time!"

Sixty years have passed away
yet one whiff of muguet* thrusts
me back to happy childhood play.

*Pronounced MEWzhay, a lily-of-the-valley perfume.

## COME BACK MARIA MONTEZ

When I was ten, I wanted to be
Maria Montez, Queen of the B movies.

On Saturday matinees, after an episode
of "Don Winslow of the Navy," Maria
slithered across the screen on some exotic
isle, in exotic dress, in erotic dance;
best was "Maria Montez in *Snake Woman!*"

Amid hooting boys, hushing ushers,
tossed popcorn, and candy wrappers,
the pink and white Good & Plenties
half-chewed—my little brother emptying
the cardboard box—I sat in a trance.

Maria, as priestess in a temple with blazing
braziers and plates of fruit ripe as her breasts,
brought in a basket and lifted the lid
to reveal her snakes, who slid out to wrap
her rippling arms, mesmerizing men.

To my skinny self, Maria had everything:
voluptuous beauty, power over men,
the woman I wanted to be when I was ten.
"Show me," my father said when I relayed the glories
of Maria's dance. I made snaky moves with thin arms,

and he, clever fellow, crafter of marionettes,
carved a puppet, designed a control stick
with wires that, when rolled under the fingers,
made the doll's arms undulate like a snake;
strings to the hips, as usual, let her sway.

Dressed in silk scraps, beads and turban,
renamed Scherezade, she joined the village
of puppet-people he'd made, with sets and stage,
to delight his only daughter; I thought all men
must be as kind and generous as he.

The Snake Goddess phase took new form when
I grew breasts and gave up sticks and strings
for ballroom steps, folk reels, square partner swings,
swirling scarves, hula skirts, and belly rolls—
the subtle arts to win the hearts of men.

But live hearts are not blocks of wood; pulling
strings to change lovers, I saw one man beat his brow
upon the floor, another weeping when I shut his door.
Yet later, even constant love could not keep from
death my father or my mate. Heartbreak . . . heartbreak.

"Come back, Maria Montez," I want to say,
"It's true about woman's power to charm
but you left out the part about power to harm."
It was much simpler then, when I was ten,
to dance with snakes.

*My brother and me looking at some of our father's hand-carved marionettes.*

## THE HOUSE ON WILLOW GROVE AVENUE

The hateful house of teenage years
became the setting for later
dreams, drenched in fears.

Where thick stone walls secreted
perpetual chills and damp mold
oozed multiple ills,
I'd wander still in the cold,
seeking something
missing.

I sensed it must
lie below the trash,
or be hid by choking dust
in a closet stash
or under a stair,
yet, *where*
I could not discover.

In the cellar sat the rat trap;
in the attic hung the wasp nest;
at risk of bites and stings
I sought, in dream after dream,
until I found the things
under the clutter—
the blue urn, and last,
the rare painting
waiting
within my past.

*December, 2006*

*My brother took this photograph of me behind a web at the Rose Art Museum at Brandeis University during an exhibition in 2005 called "DreamingNow." According to the catalogue, the artist intended that the cords connecting several beds conveyed the multiple links between dreamers in sleep.*

# Spells and Ancient Songs

Most of the poems in this section are loosely related to dream imagery, being based more on the mood of certain dreams rather than on specific images. "To the Dream Goddesses" is an exception in that the names of the divinities came in a dream depicting a distinctive invocation with ritual gestures that has never lost its mystical glow for me.

C. G. Jung once said, in *Man's Search for Meaning*, that many standard religious figures have lost much of their power to move the worshipper. He suggested that new images with the ability to inspire and guide individuals might come from our "big" dreams, the numinous few that shake us to our very core.

"The Mirror of Isis" is founded on an ancient practice of present-ing two mirrors as votive offerings at a temple of Isis in order to obtain a dream that will guide the dreamer, heal him or her, or grant fertility to a childless woman.

The Chinese brush paintings of a butterfly, a rose, and a mirror come from my book *Pathway*. They are frequent symbols of a spiritual connection in fairy tales and legends as well as in dreams.

## SPELL TO CALL A SOUL MATE

One hair to call a soul mate,
two hairs to wynd him to her side,
three hairs to bynd him. His fate:
to take her as his bride.

Daughter of Hathor plucks three hairs,
links them into a love knot,
croons a name over it thrice,
and breathes upon the spot.

She licks the hair as she twynes
it round her finger,
fynding him, bynding him fast
to her side, for all tyme.

The spell is cast!
Ah, but she will be kind . . .

*2006*

## I'VE WORN GARMENTS
### After Langston Hughes

---

I've worn garments:
I've worn garments older than linen shrouds,
as finely woven as the skin that wraps human flesh.

My soul has grown translucent like old cloth.

I draped my body in gauze with gold thread when
Isis was Queen of Heaven.

I climbed the steps, my pale limbs wrapped in a sari,
to the drum-thrumming temple of Kali.

In the Hall of Virgins, I wore a gown of voile
while feeding the Vestal flame with holy oil.

Through the dense incense, in the candlelit space
of the church of the Madonna, I paced
clad in crimson silk that rivaled velvet
cloaks on statues of the saints.

I've worn garments,
archaic, fragile garments.

My soul has grown translucent like old cloth.


*December, 2006*

## To the Dream Goddesses

To the Dream Goddesses in flight,
an entreaty for inner sight:

Come Loga, goddess bright,
let wisdom light our dreams tonight.

Come Shana, goddess fair
fill our dreams with glories rare.

Twin sister spirits of the skies,
bring us beauty, make us wise.

Blend your gifts to guide our way;
live anew in us each day.

*2005*

## THE MIRROR OF ISIS
## From Egypt

I am the Queen of Heaven, Isis;
ten thousand stars create my dress.
Every earthly mirror
is a miniature
of my silver disc in space;
I hold aloft its shining face.

If you gift two mirrors at my shrine
I will accept them as your sign.
Before my altar, at my feet, lay
down at the end of day.

Lift one moon-mirror and gaze deep
until your image clouds, then sleep.
If you've come with faith and awe,
if you'll buff away each flaw,
in a dream I will reply.
I'll grant you ease from stress,
bring you love or happiness,
or hope to the childless.

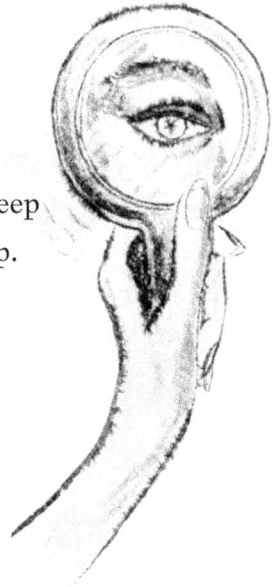

Are you worthy for this quest?
If your response is yes, come to me!
I am Great Mother Isis,
I can bless.

*December, 2006*

*Zal took this silhouette of me in the sunset on the Greek island of Mykonos in 1972.*

# Next?

When the worst of mourning has passed and the survivor has accepted loss as part of life's journey it is still not clear what the future holds, beyond the certainty of one's own death.

Yet, humor and pleasure slowly become possible again. We find we can meet even absurd frustrations with a wry smile. We can move on, treasuring what we had and staying open to what is here, now. We can live fully in the present, while occasionally glancing back and casting forward. It's not yet dark, but evening is coming soon. I explore some of these feelings in the poems in this final section.

## First Date: A Foursome?

Since this is our first date, I want to state
that I believe in open relationships.

You look puzzled; I'll explain: my ex-wife
took a long time to accept my girlfriend
into the household. After she did,
it was fine—although she still cried—

what a distraction from my work that was!
Anyway, in a few years she sued for divorce,
but who cared, I planned to wed my girlfriend . . .
until she got weird, too.

In the end, I moved in with a male friend.
We had a fabulous time . . . until
he got a disease and died. Sad.
Now, don't worry, *I'm* well!

I hope this doesn't bother you! It does?
Hmm. So, what if we just do things together,
go to movies, museums, art shows?
O.K.? And see how it goes.

I really, really like you.
You're smart enough for me,
you're sensitive enough for me.
I want a relationship with you.

Now, tell me about your experiences
with women. No interest? None?!
I see. You're a 'good girl.' Too bad.
We could have had fun.

Well, here's your house. Think
about it. I'll call you tomorrow . . .

*November, 2006*

## FIRST DATE: MAN WITH A PLAN

Ever ridden in a Maserati before? It's one
of the perks of my work. Ever eaten here
at Chez Anton?

While we're waiting for the main course,
I want to explain why you can't
move in with me.

See, my Ex says if there's any sign that
a woman's been inside, the kid can never
visit again.

Understand? Give me your hand;
here's the plan: in five years when
my kid's grown,

I'm moving to Nevada to buy a house
of my own—that dame still drives
me loco—

she'll warp the kid's mind if I don't comply
. . . just like my mom who'd act nice then
let me down.

And the last woman I dated—the one
who gave me gray hair—she saw other
men on the sly.

I love holding your hands! I'm getting
to know you. You'd never lie to me?
Ask you anything?

O.K., hmm . . . will you ever remove
the photos of your dead husband
from the wall?

You will some day, but he'll always
stay in your heart? Huh! I thought so.
Check! Waiter, check!
Let's go . . .

*December, 2006*

# First Date: Italian Lunch

"Signora, this man is not for you!
It's hard to explain why."

Toni shakes his head, sighs,
then finally he says . . .

"These new guys
you bring to my restaurant,
each one I see. Trust me,
this man is not for you."

Another sigh . . .

"Look, there is spagett, no sauce.
There is spagett with sauce—
tomate, garlic, basilique.
This man . . . *no sauce!*"

Pass the sauce, please.

*April, 2007*

# HOT NEWS

Their tryst was on a sultry Saturday in summer;
they met at his consulting office, cool and private,
where he spread the day's newspaper on the burgundy
leather couch to protect it from their heat.

When it was time to go home, she washed up
in the powder room; glancing in the mirror on the door
she saw, spread across her behind, the morning's
huge headlines, in reverse, "Fire in Philly!"

He, responding to her squeal, saw the broadside
blazoned across her backside, and laughing
so hard their ribs ached, they scrubbed away
the evidence of the afternoon's escapade.

She, like the old joke, black and white and "read"
all over; he, full of tenderness, kissed goodbye until
next time. They traveled home to waiting mates,
keeping mute about the latest hot news.

*December, 2006*

## WORKING STIFFS

Working stiffs in sturdy clothes
may tote a stick as firm
as those of gentlemanly ilk,
wearing suits of finest silk.

Thus, all wise women swear
it's not the outer clothes
that make the man—
it's his underwear.

*February, 2005*

## Beware the Charming Rat

Beware the charming rat—
he comes in many a form:
he may be thin or fat,
whip-smart or just norm.

Tall or short, light or dark of hair,
of his changing shapes, take care;
he'll use you, then lose you—
blatantly unfair!

It'd be easy to despise him,
to wrench him from your head,
if only he were not so very,
*very* good in bed.

*February, 2005*

# INDEX TO FIRST LINE
# OF POEMS

# ABOUT THE AUTHOR

**Patricia Garfield, Ph.D., is one of the world's leading** dream experts. She holds a doctorate in clinical psychology and is the author of eleven books on dreams.

Her first hook, the bestseller *Creative Dreaming,* is considered a classic. It has been in print continuously since first published (1974) and appears in fifteen languages. Her work for teens, *The Dream Book,* is the non-fiction winner of the Parents' Guide Media Award for 2002.

One of six co-founders of the International Association for the Study of Dreams, Dr. Garfield served as president during 1998-99. She is a frequent guest on American national television and radio (including three appearances on ABC's 20/20 news magazine show; three on ABC's Good Morning America; and two on CNN), as well as shows aired in Britain, Canada, Denmark, France, Germany, Sweden, and Japan. Her popular website (www.CreativeDreaming.org) has visitors from around the world. She consults for broadcasting networks in the U.S., Canada, Britain, and for U.S. film directors.

Dr. Garfield's Ph.D. in Clinical Psychology (1968) is from Temple University in Philadelphia. She taught psychology at Temple; at the Philadelphia College of Textiles and Science; at California State College, Sonoma; and at various campuses of the University of California Extension. Currently, Dr. Garfield teaches dream classes for seniors at Dominican University of California, San Rafael, California, in the Osher Lifelong Learning Institute (OLLI) program.

Having recorded her dreams for more than sixty-five years, Dr. Garfield has perhaps created the longest dream journal extant.

Books

by

Patricia Garfield, Ph.D.

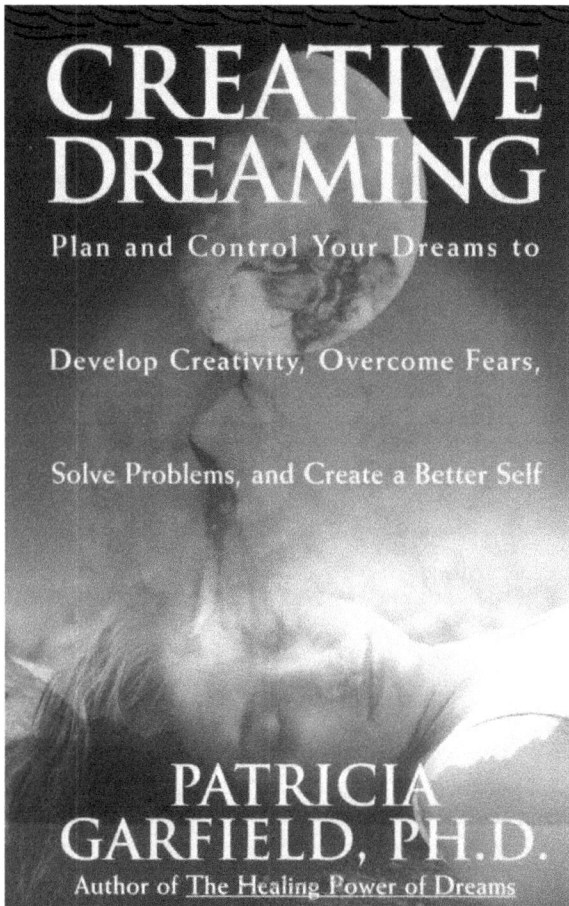

Dreams are more than just random images that play in your head at night. They are a source of inspiration and transformation that can have a profound effect on your waking state. While everyone dreams, not everyone makes use of this unique resource. Patricia Garfield presents techniques and information, drawn from many dreamers and widely varied cultures and times, that will enable you to plan your dreams ahead of time, influence them while they are occurring, and recall them and their lessons forever afterward.

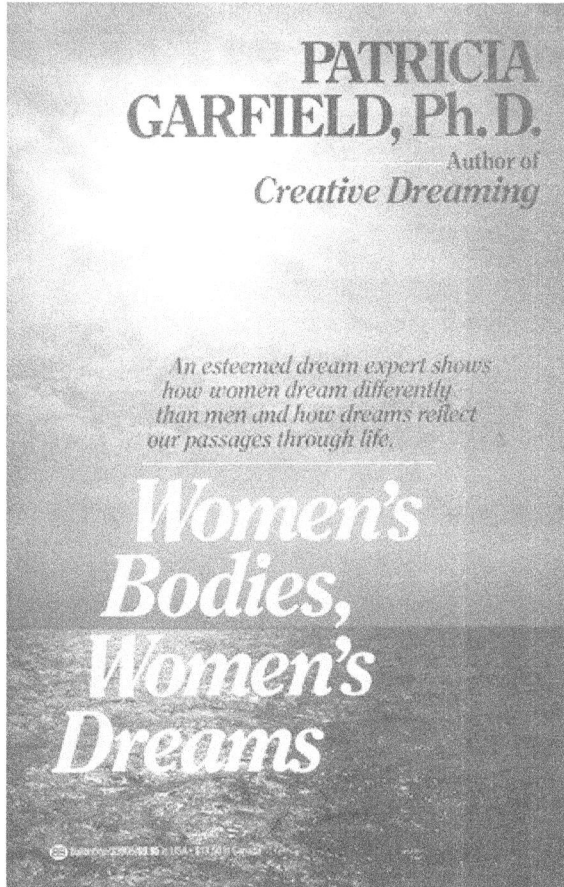

PATRICIA
GARFIELD, Ph.D.
Author of
*Creative Dreaming*

An esteemed dream expert shows
how women dream differently
than men and how dreams reflect
our passages through life.

*Women's*
*Bodies,*
*Women's*
*Dreams*

An emotional and spiritual journey through the seasons of a woman's life, this illuminating book reveals, chapter-by-chapter, the role dreams play in each stage of a woman's development—and how they can help her adjust healthily and calmly to her changing body and emotional state. Here, too, are the recurrent dream symbols that appear with each new life passage—and what they mean. Compelling and enlightening, this book provides the prescription for understanding our dreams, our bodies, our lives. Written by a dream expert with the most extensive dream log ever recorded—over 20,000 in all—it will guide the way to well-being and emotional health for women everywhere.

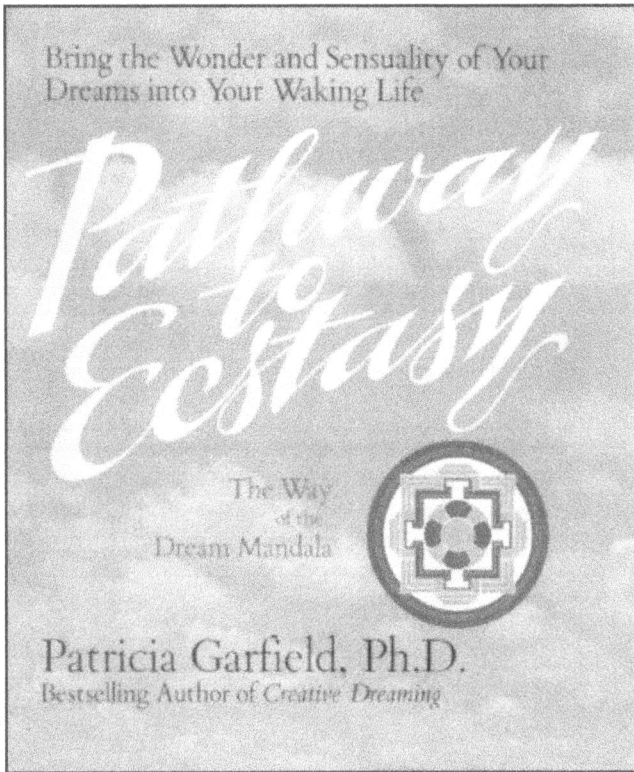

Bring the Wonder and Sensuality of Your
Dreams into Your Waking Life

*Pathway
to
Ecstasy*

The Way
of the
Dream Mandala

Patricia Garfield, Ph.D.
Bestselling Author of *Creative Dreaming*

Patricia Garfield, author of the classic bestseller, *Creative Dreaming*, candidly reveals her own rich, sensual journey through a lifetime of dreaming and shows you how to chart your own pathway to ecstasy.

Garfield uses as her guide the sacred Tibetan mandala—a circle or group that is organized symmetrically around its center. As you become more aware of your dreams and learn how to remember, interpret, and even direct them, the mandala becomes a pathway through various levels of consciousness to mystic union with the center, the vibrant core within us all, the source of all life. Approaching the center of the mandala, you become your own guide on the road to spiritual transcendence and sexual fulfillment.

PATRICIA GARFIELD, Ph.D.
Author of *Creative Dreaming*

The Dream Book

A YOUNG PERSON'S GUIDE
TO UNDERSTANDING DREAMS

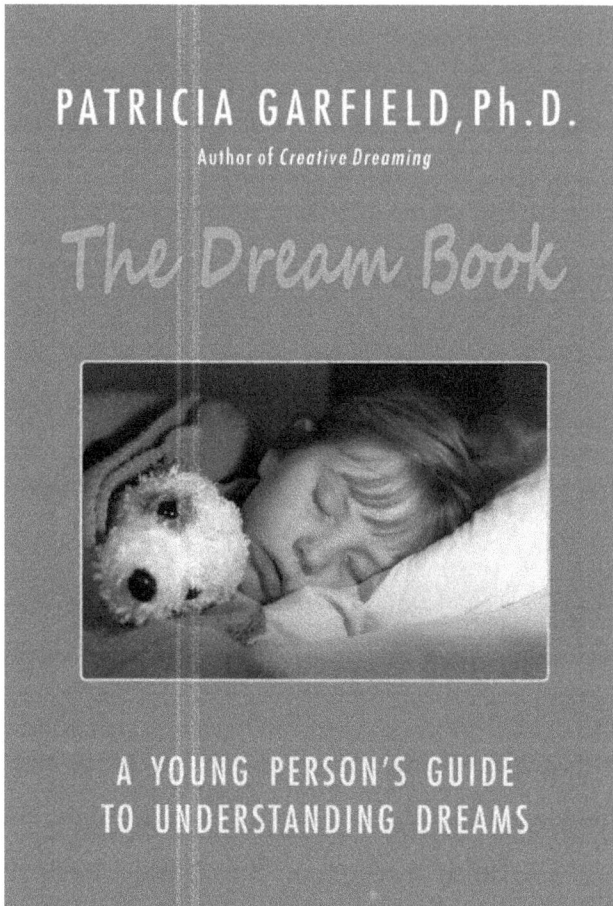

People have long been fascinated by the meaning of dreams. In fact, young people around the world have similar dreams. World-renowned dream expert Patricia Garfield has gathered together the common types of dreams – dreams of being chased, of unfinished homework, of falling, even of being undressed in the most awkward places – and helps young people understand their dreams. She gives excellent suggestions to help young readers remember these dreams and influence them so that they become a source of insight.

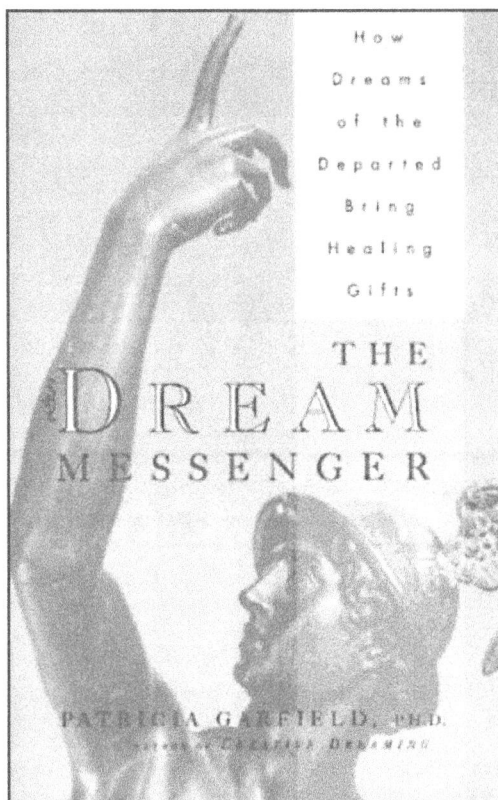

*The Dream Messenger: How Dreams of the Departed Bring Healing Gifts* continues Dr. Patricia Garfields's tradition of exploring how dreams can function as tools for healing in our waking lives. The Dream Messenger focuses on dreams of the dead — identifying several components of such dream encounters, and providing techniques for integrating these dreams with bereavement and re-awakening to life after the loss of a loved one. Based on a study of hundreds of dreams of people during grief, as well as her own journals and the writings of other contemporary authors, Garfield brings a rich sense of shared emotion and human experience to the grieving process, and to the need to integrate our continuing relationships with those who have died.

# THE Healing Power OF Dreams

TECHNIQUES FOR INTERPRETING
AND USING YOUR DREAMS TO:
REVEAL HIDDEN HEALTH PROBLEMS,
SPEED YOUR RECOVERY,
AND PROMOTE LIFELONG HEALTH

Patricia Garfield, Ph.D.
AUTHOR OF *CREATIVE DREAMING*

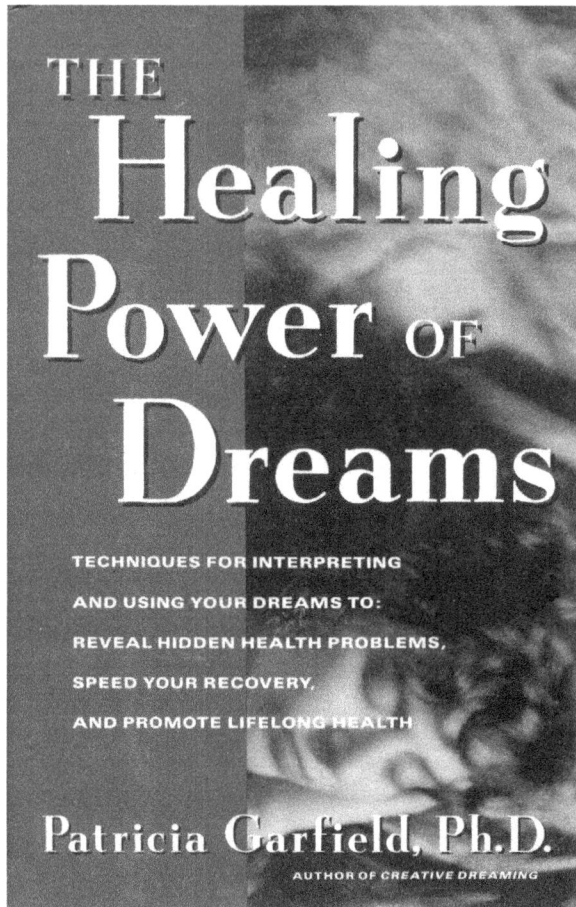

The first book to describe in detail the practical application of dreams in healing, this breakthrough guide explains how to identify dreams that may warn of health problems. Dr. Garfield shows how to transform unhealthy dream images into healthy ones, release trauma by recording dreams, and use visualization of dream imagery to accelerate healing. Includes twelve line drawings.

The
Universal
Dream
Key

The 12 Most Common Dream
Themes Around the World

PATRICIA GARFIELD, PH.D.
Author of the Bestseller
*CREATIVE DREAMING*

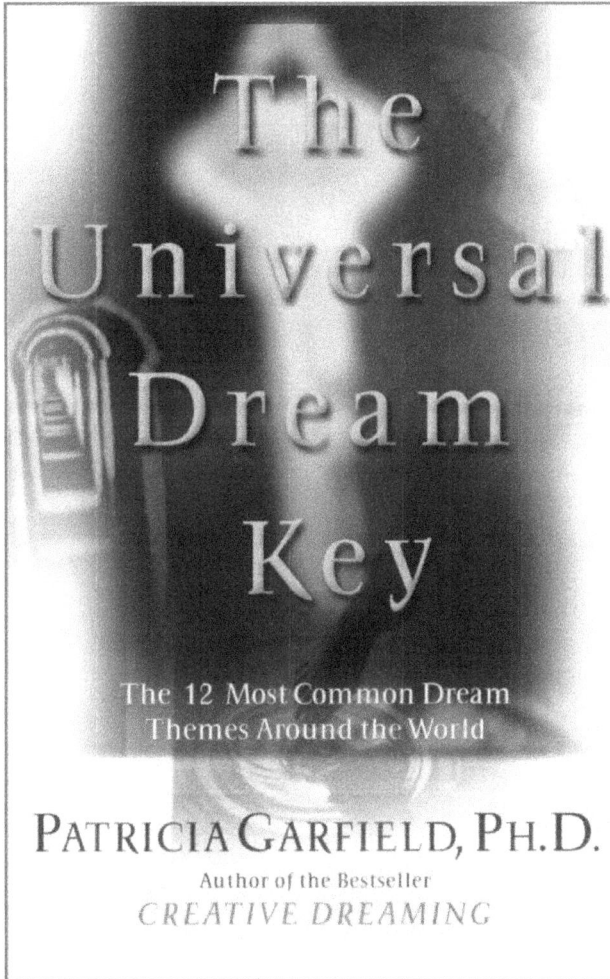

Every night, all over the world, sleepers are dreaming variations of the same twelve dreams. The details differ, of course, but the same themes recur in every culture, as they have throughout recorded history. In *The Universal Dream Key*, internationally renowned authority Dr. Patricia Garfield shows us how to understand our dreams — and learn much about ourselves.

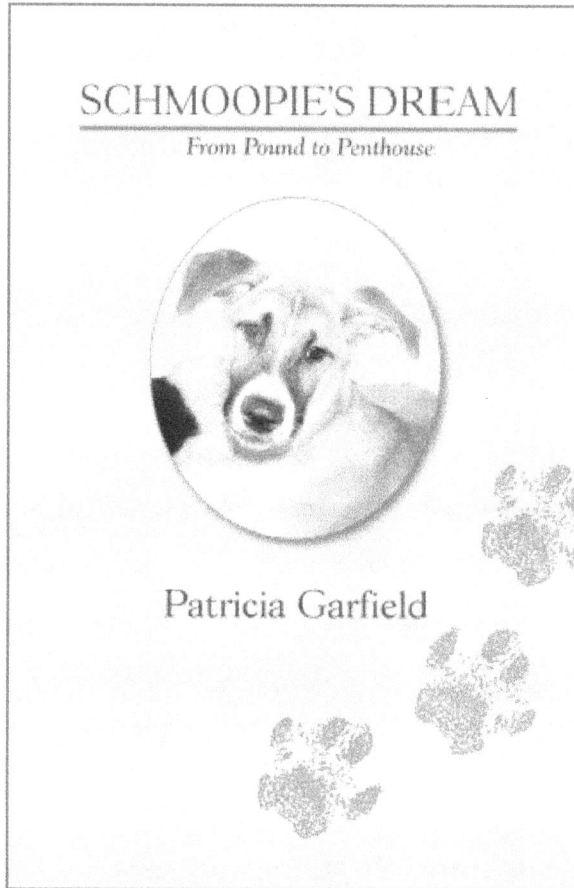

Dr. Patricia Garfield's new book for children. Published in 2014. Available via www.creativedreaming.org and on Amazon.com.

*When Schmoopie, the runt and sole survivor of a litter, is rescued from the pound, her wish for a new family is fulfilled beyond her wildest dreams.*

www.ingramcontent.com/pod-product-compliance
Lightning Source LLC
Chambersburg PA
CBHW071021040426
42443CB00007B/882